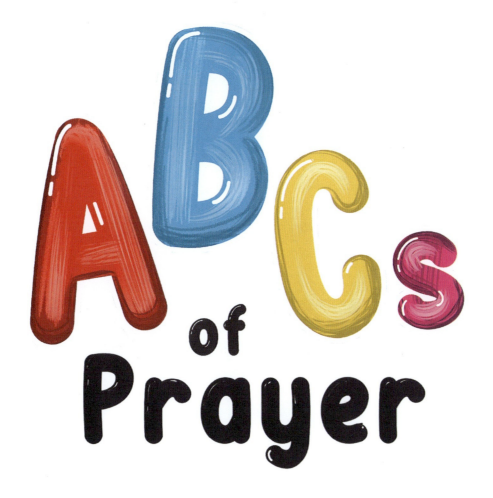

Written by:
Sunny Kang &
Anna Kim Kang

Illustrated by:
Alexandro Ockyno &
Ruth Handayani

Text and Illustrations Copyright © 2022 Sunny Kang and Anna Kim Kang
All rights reserved. No part of this publication may be reproduced, distributed, or transmitted in any form or by any means, including photocopying, recording, or other electronic or mechanical methods, without the prior written permission of the publisher, except in the case of brief quotations embodied in reviews and certain other non-commercial uses permitted by copyright law. The moral right of the author and illustrator has been asserted.

Ebook: 978-1-958879-88-7
Paperback: 978-1-958879-87-0
Hardcover: 978-1-958879-89-4

May your family learn the joys and power of prayer!

To :

_____

From :

_____

Date :

_____

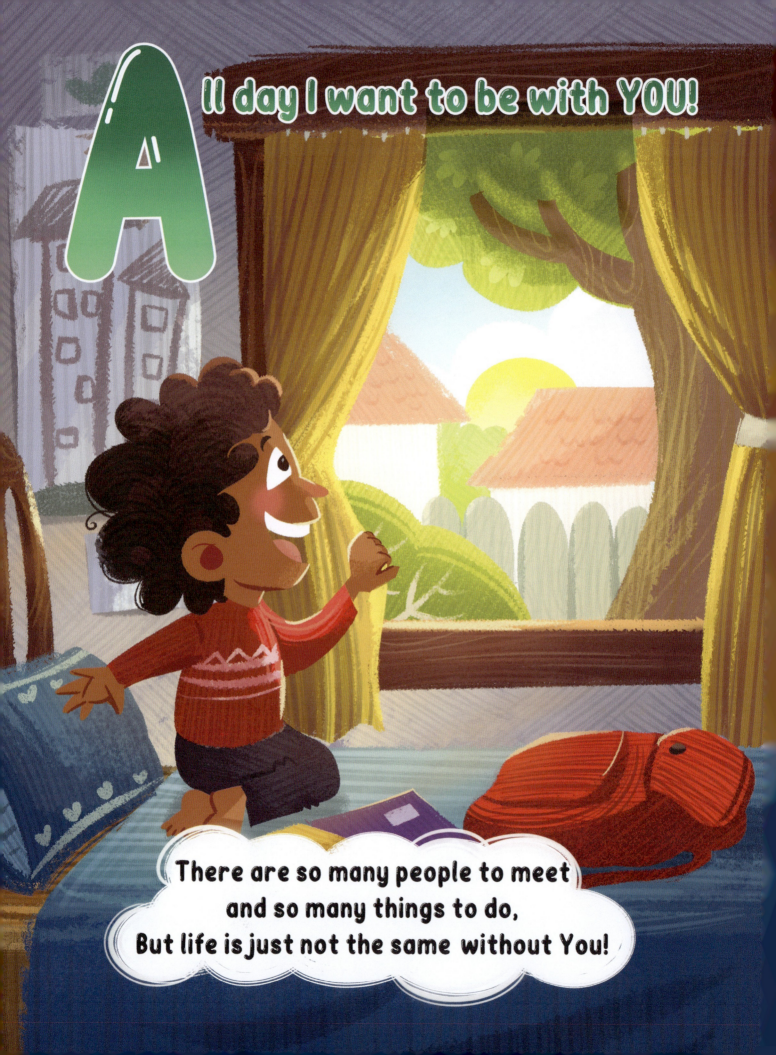

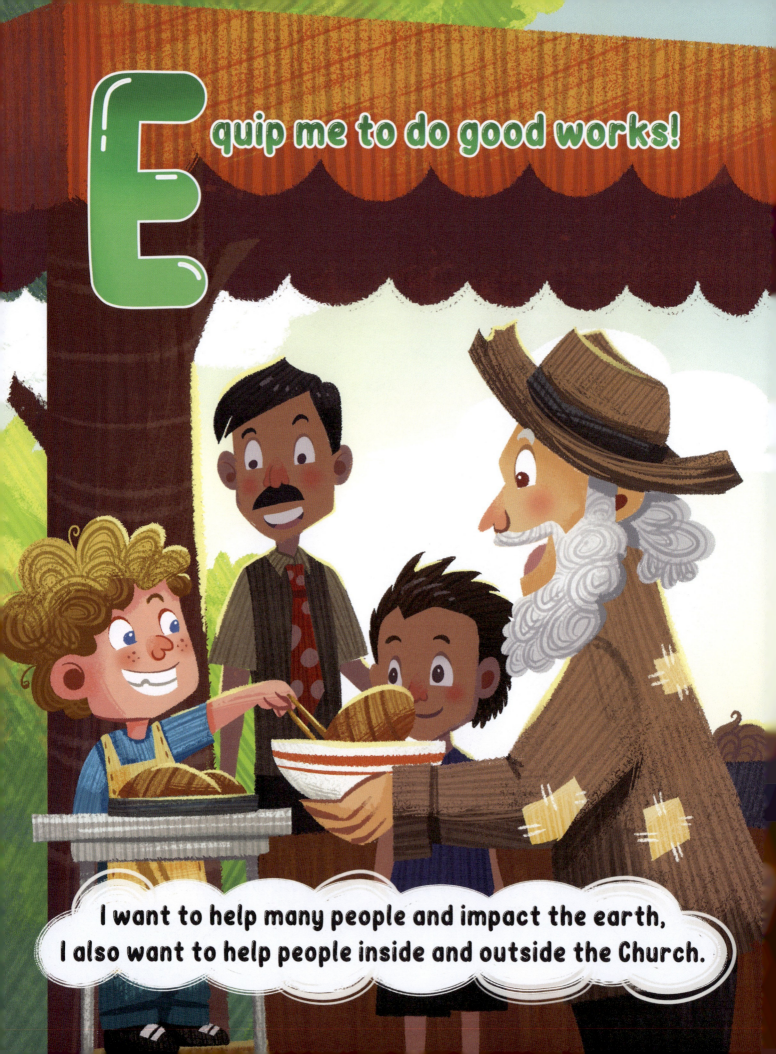

Heal my friend in Jesus' name!

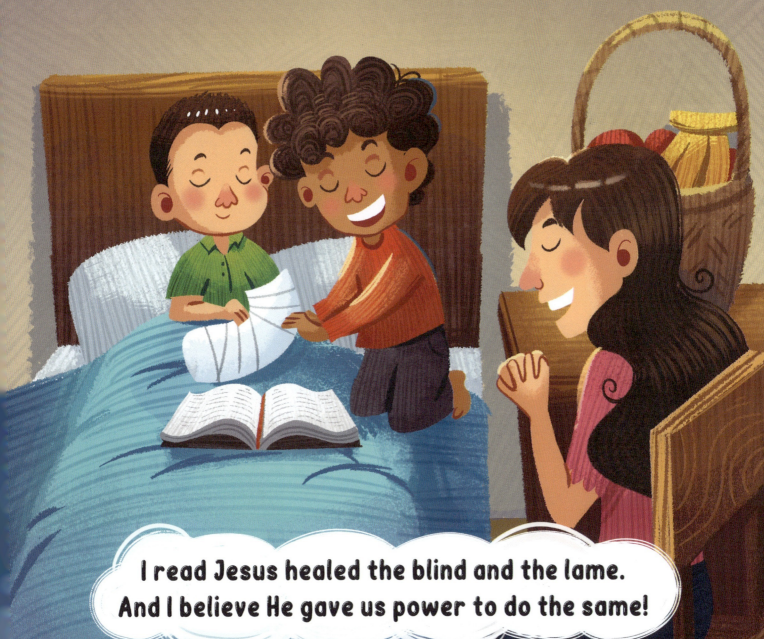

I read Jesus healed the blind and the lame.
And I believe He gave us power to do the same!

I love You!

3-A

You know everything I think and everything I do,
I cannot escape Your love and would never try to.

Jesus is so amazing!

He came to earth as a humble and amazing King,
Showed us how to live by faith, while not complaining.

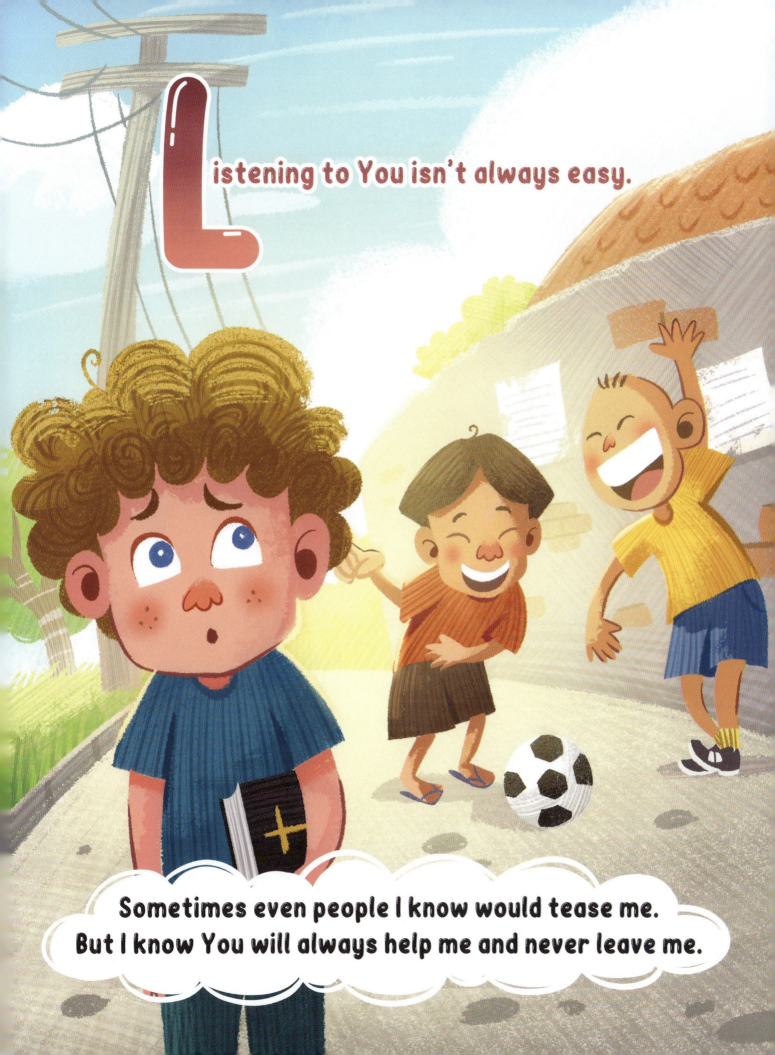

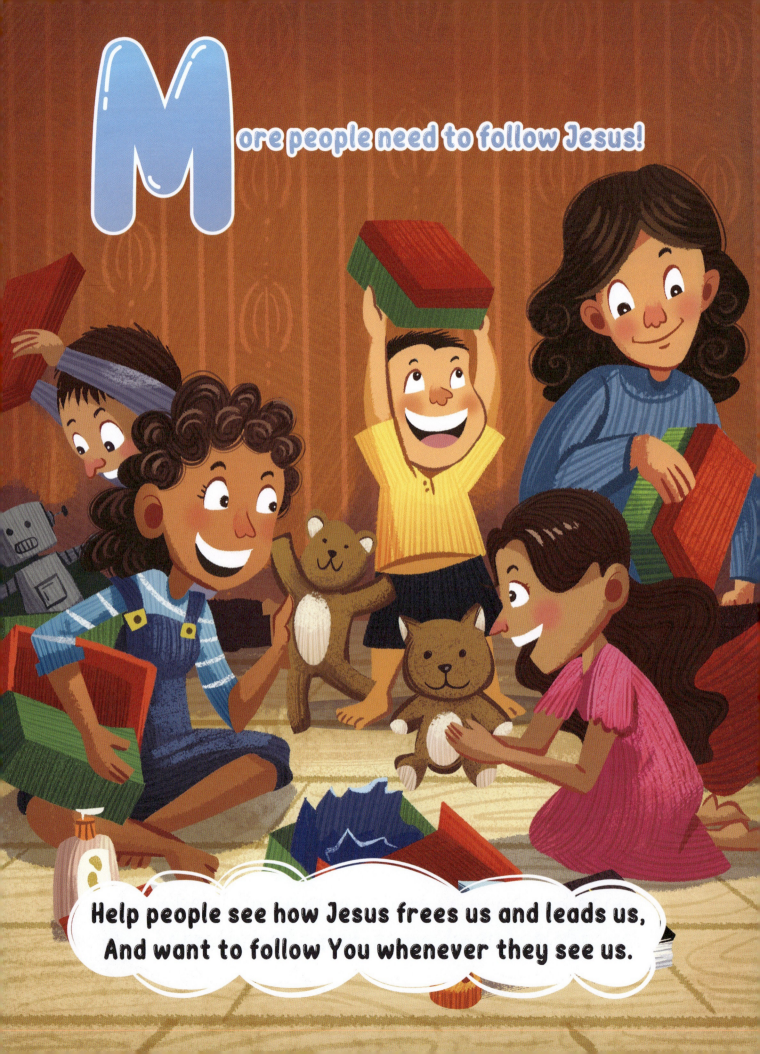

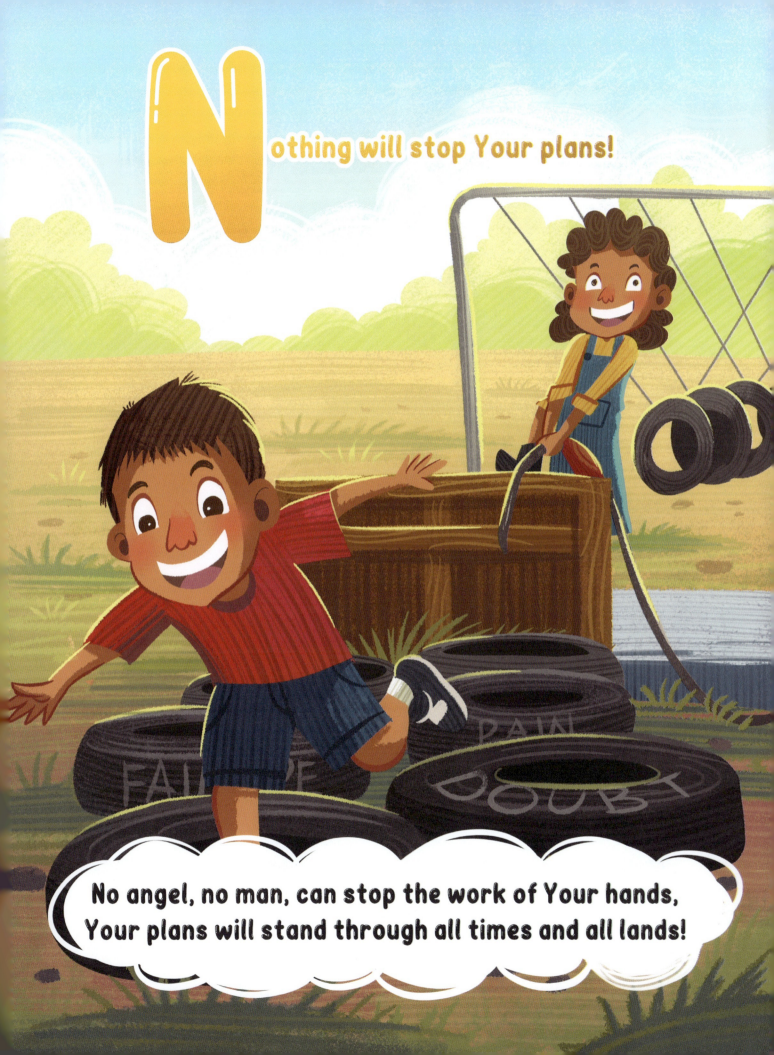

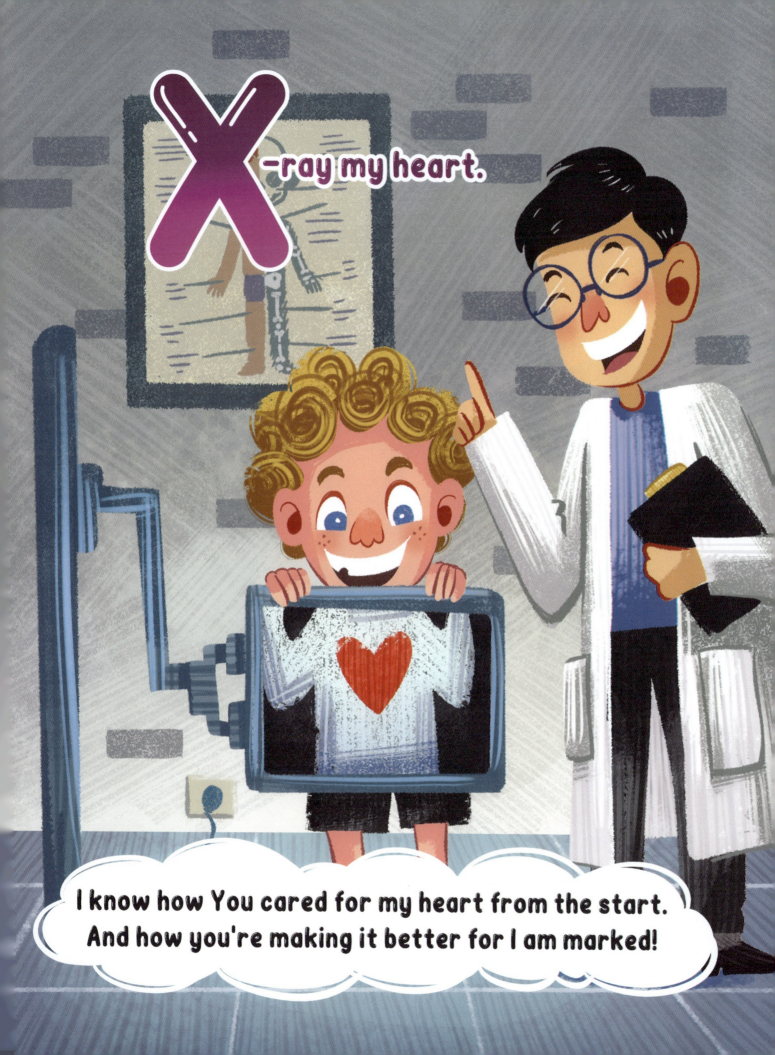

Your Kingdom come, Your will be done!

Jesus showed Your heavenly ways to everyone. So may Your will be done through Your daughters and sons.

ABOUT THE AUTHORS

Sunny Kang is a Christ follower, husband, father, teacher, preacher, and author. He has pastored for over 10 years, serving as children's pastor for several of those years. He enjoys learning, meeting new people, communicating God's Word, superhero movies, and boba! He, his wife, and 2 sons live and serve in Las Vegas.

Anna Kim Kang is a wife and mother of two amazing boys. She enjoys coffee, boba, ice cream, and all things sweet. She desires to create a better world for her two sons and future generations.

FOLLOW AUTHOR :
Facebook @AuthorSunnyKang | Instagram @AuthorSunnyKang
Email: sunnykang@e3books.com

ABOUT THE ILLUSTRATORS

Alexandro Ockyno is a full-time freelance illustrator, living in Bali for almost 9 years. He created Cat and Sashimi Art Studio as his passion is 2D illustrations. He dreams of making art for children and to share God's blessings with many others.

FOLLOW ILLUSTRATOR :
Facebook @alessandro.altobelly | Instagram @alexandrooukino
Art Studio Instagram @catandsashimi

Ruth Handayani, a girl who loves to dive in her imagination. She is a full-time illustrator, living in Bali for almost 10 years.
She believes becoming a children's illustrator is God's calling. So she wants to create children's illustrations to share God's blessings and to fill many people with joy.

FOLLOW ILLUSTRATOR :
Facebook @Ruth Handayani | Instagram @ruthxhandayani
Art Studio Instagram @catandsashimi

Check Out More Bible Seminary Series Books!

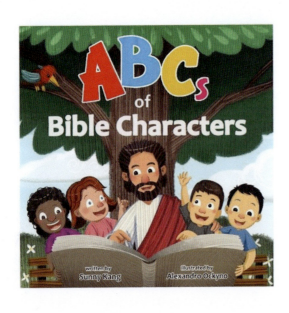 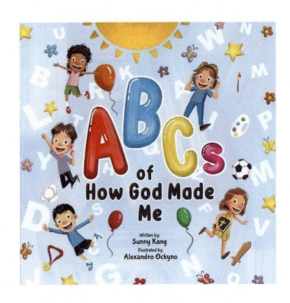

Amazon.com

Enjoy this book?
Please leave a review!

Christian School Curriculum Available Now!

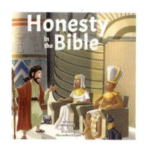

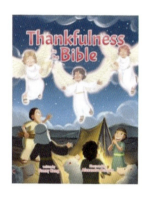
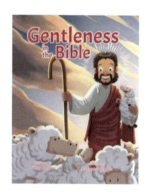
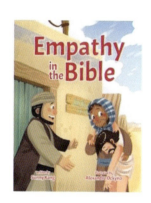
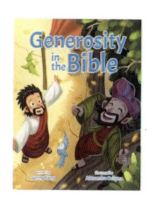

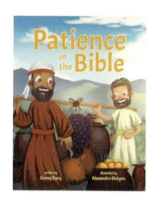

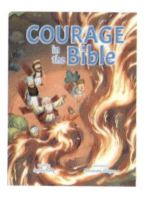

For bulk orders contact:
sunnykang@e3books.com